THE NATURAL HIGH

THE NATURAL HIGH

Secrets to Overcoming Instant Gratification and Finding Inner Peace

M.K HIEMANN

The Centre for Healing

Copyright © 2022 by Melissa K Hiemann

Credits
Front Cover: Melissa K Hiemann
Editing: Fiona Spinks
Photograph: Finn McAleer
Preface Mention: Ryan Hassan

All rights reserved. No part of this book may be reproduced in any manner whatsoever without written permission except in the case of brief quotations embodied in critical articles and reviews.

Ebook ISBN: 978-0-6489460-0-7
Print ISBN: 978-0-6489460-1-4
First Printing, 2020

Publisher - **The Centre for Healing**

CONTENTS

	DEDICATION	vii
1	Preface	1
2	What is a Natural High?	7
3	What is in The Way of The Natural High?	15
4	What Are We Really Addicted to?	21
5	Trauma Bonding	30
6	Just Coping	37
7	Labels: The Life Sentence	43
8	Clearing The Blocks	49
9	Healing Trauma	57
10	Follow	68

CONTENTS

11 | The Ripple Effect   74

12 | Bigger Issue   80

13 | Consciousness   84

14 | Attainment   90

15 | Longevity   96

16 | The Future   102

17 | Relax   109

JOURNAL EXERCISE   115
JOURNAL   119
NOTES   123
ABOUT THE AUTHOR   124

> To my dear father Fred. Without you I wouldn't be where I am today.
> Rest in peace.

Preface

The moment Ryan walked in, I struggled to hide my shock. I was immediately taken aback and, for a moment, felt fear in not knowing what to do. The man that I remembered from a year ago as being 15kg heavier and much healthier, had just walked into my office looking deteriorated, with clothes tattered - almost unrecognisable. I was worried for a moment and was almost going to call my friend, who had just walked out, to come back and help me.

But a voice in my mind said with certainty: "You can do this".

I had met Ryan a year prior at a local doctor's clinic during a talk that had been set up by a mutual acquaintance. He was talking about nutrition, and I was talking about the effects of stress. We hit it off pretty quickly and caught up for a drink not long after. He told me he had just found out that his wife was leaving him and had been cheating on him. I offered a listening ear but had also just become a therapist and was trying to get him to have a session with me - it was the only way that I knew how to help him at the time.

We caught up again, he came to visit my practice and co- working space in beach-side Melbourne, and he gave me a few samples of a health product that he was selling at the time.

That was the last time I saw him for almost a year...

The day prior to Ryan coming in, almost a year later, I was sitting on Facebook and saw him come up on my chat as being active online. Again, I hadn't seen or heard from him for a long time, so this came as quite a surprise. I said hello and asked how he had been and what he had been up to.

I had recently learnt a method of remote healing, and practicing what I had been taught, I tuned into him, into his energy field so to speak. I felt a sharp pain in my heart, and I told him this. He immediately responded and said that, yes, he had been struggling - so much so he "could write a book about what had been happening in the year or so since I had seen him". Intrigued, but also wanting to help, I asked him to write down with his non- dominant hand all of the negative emotions he was feeling. I was still unaware of what had gone on, and he knew I was a therapist of some sort, but he didn't really know what I did. He started writing but confessed that he didn't know how to deal with what was coming up.

He asked if he could book a session with me ASAP. What I didn't know was that he had promised his family and friends he would see a counsellor that week, but accidently missed his appointment the day before. They were putting pressure on him, and he was putting pressure on himself to show that he was getting help. He had gone deep into an Ice (methamphetamine) and GHB addiction and had lost contact with them, while living in a drug den and dealing drugs with his then-girlfriend, to support their use.

I checked my schedule, but didn't have much availability that week, although I sensed urgency when he pleaded for a session the next day. Not long after his request, I had a cancellation come through from another client and, thankfully, fit him in. Little did I know this would be a turning point in both our lives.

He came into my office and sat down. I had a cliche, long, white, day lounge-style therapy chair, and asked him to take a seat. He sat down, hunched over, and looking at the ground. I was trying not to judge him, but it was such a far cry from the man I remembered - tanned, muscly, well-dressed, with an air of confidence. He could hardly look at me as we started. I told him how the session would run and asked him to share with me what had brought him in that day. "For the past 8-9 months I have been using ice and GHB daily", he said.

I didn't skip a beat - at least it made it clearer to me why he was in the physical state he was in. I explained what he was addicted to (aside from the drugs) and why he needed something to cope, by showing him The Scale of Consciousness by Dr David Hawkins, and to extend on our conversation from the day prior about the emotions that were coming up for him.

He seemed to understand but said he was feeling a little out of it as he had used earlier that day. A picture flashed up in my mind of the ice rages that are depicted in the media, but for some reason a part of me felt I would be safe. I asked him to stand up so we could work through the process of checking his beliefs on a subconscious level, revealing what may have led him down this road to avoid his feelings, or to 'cope'. He seemed a little confused but somewhat trusting of the process - like it was his last chance to redeem himself. He laid back down on the sofa, and I put on the meditation music and started the healing process.

The session went for nearly 3 hours.

At the end, he was just staring at the wall. I looked into his eyes and said, "Better than any drug, isn't it?", to which he replied, "1000 times better than any drug that I have ever had!" He then told me he had felt totally present for the first time in his whole life.

A few months and sessions later, I received a voice message from Ryan. "Mel, I need you to teach me every single thing that you know! I don't care how long it takes or what I have to do!" I was slightly taken aback, but at the same time felt honoured he would ask me.

Since seeing me for ongoing sessions, he had recovered and found his purpose. He signed up for a Diploma in AOD (alcohol and other drugs) as he told me he had a vision that he would open up a centre to assist others in their recovery. But after a few classes, and a few arguments with his teacher as to when they would start talking about and healing the root causes of why someone was using, his frustration and burning vision to open his own clinic led him back to me. He asked me to be his teacher. It felt like a real 'Mr. Miyagi' moment for me, and it was great timing. The day after that first intense healing session, an air conditioner under my office had energy run to it for the first time in five years and ended up catching fire, burning the whole building down. I'd been practicing out of my apartment, and it was becoming unsustainable. Since I became certified, I had spent day and night studying in between sessions - even moving in with two other healers and studying with them for nine months - so thankfully I had a lot of information and knowledge to share and pass on.

In Ryan's words, he turned into a house hermit for the next four

months. He laughed, thinking his housemate thought he may be going crazy, with piles of books around him, weird quotes on the walls, and binaural beats music pumping constantly in the background.

A far cry from glass pipes and defrosting GHB on his electric heater.

Now Ryan and I are a couple, and we have a gorgeous son Tommy Brave. We opened that centre with nothing but have created a team and the healing centre that we both dreamed of. Once Tommy came into our lives, our priorities shifted and we are currently 'digital nomads', travelling full-time (for now) and conducting online healing sessions, as well as teaching others the methods that changed our lives and those of countless others.

M.K HIEMANN

> *This book is an effort to share with you what we have learnt for ourselves, the wisdom gained from overcoming our pain, and discovering ways to naturally heal from our own addictions and instant gratifications. Along with the witnessing and experiencing of many others on this journey to inner peace.*

2

What is a Natural High?

> *natural high (meaning)*
> *noun*
> *a euphoric or excited state that is not due to*
> *ingestion of drugs or another substance*

On a basic human level, we are always striving to some degree to feel good at all times. Although, of course, this is not only unobtainable but also unrealistic and it could actually be detrimental to think we could be in a constant state of happiness all the time. Because when we are not 'happy' we reject ourselves and what we cannot control in the world and cause ourselves emotional pain. A natural high is potentially what we are striving for when we are working towards and completing inner and outer goals throughout our lives. So, the distinction between happiness and a natural high needs to be made, so realistic ideals and expectations can be set early on in reading this, while deepening your understanding and attainment of the 'high', naturally. So, for the sake of distinction in this book, when we talk about a natural high, we are talking about a high-energy state with euphoric yet peaceful and balanced feelings.

The dictionary definition of a natural high is a euphoric or excited state *that is not due to the ingestion of drugs or other substances.* You may not have thought of this, but the high that you experience is actually produced because the chemicals already within our bodies are being manipulated by these outside substances. So, anything you take to induce the feeling of a high is actually just

manipulating the way your body takes up or blocks the chemicals that you already have in you, to create these states when you are 'high' or 'relaxed'. But we don't have to take a substance or an impulsive action to induce the feeling at all!

This is one of the main reasons why two people who take exactly the same drug can have two completely different responses - one may become addicted, and another person may not.

Let me give you an example of a natural high and the circumstances leading to it, so you can relate and become more aware of the possibility of creating this state on your own, for example through a recollection of past experiences. If you think you've only ever gotten high from a drug or a certain addictive behaviour, then I want to challenge you on that.

Let's say you've been feeling like going for a walk on the beach. You were just thinking about it this morning as you noticed it was a warm day. You haven't visited the beach for a while but have been meaning to. Only 30 minutes later you get a message from a friend, "Hey, what are you up to? Do you feel like coming to the beach?" You are taken aback for a moment while your mind processes what could perhaps be a coincidence or synchronicity - or the mere fact that you are excited to see that friend and you already wanted to go to the beach. You text back with excitement, "I was literally just thinking about going! Can you read my mind?!" You start thinking about the beach as you energetically grab your towel and get excited about the picture which is now being projected into your future mind, and you just cannot wait to feel the warmth on your skin and the sand between your toes - it's as if your body thinks it's already there.

Did you notice the three parts in the example? First, there was a desire in mind based on a positive past experience. Then there was a manifestation or reward for thinking of the desire (the actualisation of the desire through the friend) and lastly, there was a daydream coupled with a strong feeling of enjoyment in the present moment, physically in your body. Something like this, if they were looking forward to it, would give someone a burst of energy, a burst of feel-good chemicals and a set goal for the future.

To give you an opposing example, your body may react differently in the present moment if you were being asked to take the rubbish out, go and vote, or see someone you don't like.

On the surface level, that example may sound quite standard - but don't be deflated. We are about to talk about the 'feel-good' or 'natural high' chemicals that are involved throughout that process. They are always there as the undercurrent in our lives, we just need to understand them more deeply so we can become more aware and conscious within our bodies, and use this information to heal, change or make a new choice - things to our advantage.

Let's start with GABA (gamma-aminobutyric acid), which is an inhibitory molecule that slows down the firing of neurons and creates a sense of calmness. An increase in this chemical can reduce anxiety. In relation to our example, you were thinking about the beach and feeling how you felt by drawing on that memory. That recall slowed your mind down and allowed you to let go of the anxiety to get out of the house for that day.

Then there was the synchronicity. You had just been reminiscing about going to the beach, which created the desire, and then your friend contacted you. The excitement most likely would have given you an internal rush of adrenaline (or epinephrine), which gives you a surge of energy, giving you the ability to jump off the couch or out of bed to pack your things. Versus, say, putting the bin out, where you would have no energy, or even resistance to completing the task.

While you are packing your towel and lotion, you start imagining that you're at the beach already with your friend in your mind. This most likely will give you a hit of dopamine, the reward chemical, which drives you towards reward- driven behaviour, with another hit when you arrive.

Upon meeting the friend at the beach, you may then experience bonding and a feeling of connection. The chemical you may now be feeling is serotonin, the
confidence and happiness molecule, due to being comfortable with your friend. Or if you have a love for this person, you may feel oxytocin, the love hormone.

You then go for a long walk in the sun along the beach, which reduces stress, and the exercise releases more chemicals called endorphins.

You then hug your friend and thank them for a great time. This act of touch and connection may release more oxytocin, which is also directly linked to human bonding and increases trust and loyalty.

Every single one of the chemicals mentioned above can be artificially induced through a prescribed or illegal substance, or an addictive behaviour, with potentially negative consequences.

Personally, I prefer the beach way.

Based on the example above, let's weigh up the positives vs negatives:

Natural Way	Substance/Behaviour Way
Increased fitness and longevity	Decrease in fitness and immune system
Maintenance of friendship/connection/support	Isolation or toxic connections
Sunshine, Vitamin D increase	More likely to stay at home
A new experience to reminisce on	Memory loss and confusion due to an altered state

Stress reduction, natural relaxation	Stress increasing before and after ingestion
Low / no financial commitment	Negative effects on short and long- term financial situation

Above are just a few generalisations and examples of the difference between two outcomes of a false or induced high through addictions, rather than the natural high of chemicals in a positive experience.

What is the difference between a natural high and a false high you may ask?

A natural high is a short burst or sustained elated and blissful feeling, which brings about life-affirming and healthy consequences. A false high is categorised as an external behaviour or ingestion of a substance that results in negative consequences and is harmful to wellbeing, either directly through physical and mental issues or indirectly through financial issues and relationship loss. We are actually very capable of obtaining a natural high ourselves, such as a runner's high - feeling really good, altering our consciousness or state of mind, and feeling a positive sense of self. This is a "healthy high" compared to that received from drinking, smoking, and using drugs.

The reason I took the time to create this book to talk about my personal experiences and those of my clients experiencing this *natural high* state, is simply because there is a need for people to know, in all walks of life, that happiness, peace, and a high for life can be theirs simultaneously and naturally.

M.K HIEMANN

3

What is in The Way of The Natural High?

> *Every pain, addiction, anguish, longing, depression, anger or fear is an orphaned part of us seeking joy, some disowned shadow wanting to return to the light and home of ourselves.- Jacob Nordby*

Whenever a new client comes to our healing centre for their first session, one of the initial things we want to know is where someone wants to ideally be, in terms of their goals and how that will feel once achieved. As we delve into experiencing this reality with them - in a place in the future where all their issues and problems have miraculously gone - we find sidenotes popping up with blocks in their mind of all the reasons as to why they can't or why it couldn't be possible to achieve what they are envisioning and sharing with us.

The negative experiences of life inevitably make us emotionally heavier overtime. Just like an onion, we obtain layers and layers of experience which can distort how we see ourselves and the world. If we allow the layers to stay, then we may energetically feel heavier and heavier. We get serious, angry, cynical, depressed, or cold and start to lose the sparkle in our eyes. Sadly, we can lose the ability to see the beauty and appreciate the simple things in life, as we may have done as children. So often people talk about their current issues and pains. As therapists and healers and through the experience of seeing it over and over again, we can sense something deeper is at play as they explain their current perspectives and issues. Based on seeing countless people and helping them get past these circumstances quite quickly, we know that about 90% of the time they are actually seeing their current situation through the fogged-up lens of the past. Not only is this lens visual, which gives us a distorted perception, it is also kinaesthetic - we can *feel* it. And the lens fracture that is caused by the past experience acts like a magnet, repeating similar experiences, life patterns, and people that are like the ones who originally hurt us, as the mind and body so desperately tries to heal the original pain.

To further your understanding, let me give you an unfortunately common example. A lady comes in who doesn't understand why she has attracted another narcissistic and somewhat emotionally or physically abusive partner. Since she was a teenager, she seemingly keeps attracting these abusive and controlling men. Every time she builds up the courage to leave, she stays on her own for a while, only to find herself with another similar character. They crush her self-esteem in order to control her. Their control comes from their own feelings of insecurity, and perhaps they feel the need to do this so they don't feel powerlessness, which could be their greatest fear because of their own childhood wounds. As her self-esteem is crushed, she finally decides that it's time to love herself and seeks help by way of some support and therapy. In delving into her past, we find out her father showed a lot of the same traits and treated her in a similar way when she was growing up. A part of her, her soul or inner young child, couldn't believe someone she looked up to, trusted, and wanted the adoration of, could abuse her. A part of her shattered, or essentially broke off and was then suppressed or pushed down into the deepest parts of her mind. An 'onion' or ego layer was created to protect her, and the sparkle left her eyes. Her inner child is now shaken, distrusting and scared. But, as mentioned before, that part of her desperately wanted to be healed, desperately wanted her father to eventually say sorry, approve of her and never abuse her again.

Because it wasn't resolved or completely processed at the time, she is unconsciously still trying to mend that part through what is called *trauma bonding*, which shows up for her by being attracted to men that were similar in some way to her father. She logically wants a man to love and nurture her, but in order to heal the inner child wound she will feel pulled beyond her will to men with the same traits as her father, and she will play the abused child victim again after the honeymoon period of the relationship subsides. Subconsciously, her wounded inner child theoretically thinks that if she finally gets her current partner to stop abusing her, to say sorry and finally nurture her - then finally her inner child can now be held, healed, and feel safe so she can truly feel loved and safe in her own skin and environment again.

How does she keep attracting and being attracted to these types of people? Is it bad luck? Is it stupidity? No, it's just a lack of awareness and understanding that it's her wounded inner child trying to finally be healed by the current partner in her life.

These are the wounds and the causes of patterns in our lives. The ones that stop us from knowing why we keep attracting the same circumstances. The 'why does this keep happening to me?' events. These traumatic or painful experiences create the beliefs, negative self-talk and behaviours that limit us going forward and limit what we are capable of feeling and creating in this life. It's the root- cause of why we struggle with money, make bad decisions, excuse and even blame others, but deep down we desperately yearn and want a different situation. Why do we wish we could start our own business to live passionately every day doing something we love but are scared of what people might think and how they might judge us if it isn't successful?

Why we don't think we are good enough or have the fear of people judging us in pursuing certain studies or hobbies?

We may think that we are a good person if we fully sacrifice our life in order to help others, continuously pouring from a nearly empty cup and finding ourselves resentful, depressed, and feeling isolated when there is no reciprocity from those we help or others in general.

These layers, resentments, and perhaps the heavy pain we hold in our hearts, the anger that covers what we won't allow ourselves to let go of, such as pain and hurt from decades ago, are just a few of a long list of 'what ifs' that are blocking our way from the naturally high or peaceful state.

When the layers are too heavy and we can't find the joy in life from within anymore, we look for external comforts, like bingeing on chocolate for a taste of love and serotonin. Like alcohol, we drink to numb the anxieties of the future, for fear the pattern will repeat and we'll still be powerless against it. Like the rush of buying new clothes or a car, where the feeling fades not long after it is in our possession.

WHEN SOMEONE HAS AN ADDICTION, EVEN FROM MY OWN EXPERIENCE OF OVERCOMING MY ADDICTIONS - THERE ARE KEY FACTORS THAT ARE PLAYING A

PART. 1 - THE BOTTLED-UP EMOTIONS AND THOUGHTS THAT ARISE FROM NEGATIVE

PAST EXPERIENCES ARE TOO UNCOMFORTABLE TO SIT WITH PEACEFULLY IN

THE NOW. 2 - WHEN SOMETHING CALMS US OR HELPS US FEEL SOOTHED AND THE DIFFERENCE IS STRONG ENOUGH FROM THE NEGATIVE FEELINGS THAT WE ARE FEELING, THEN IT WILL BURN A STRONG MEMORY INTO OUR MINDS. SO

M.K HIEMANN

WHENEVER WE FEEL UNCOMFORTABLE, OUR BODY WILL QUICKLY SCAN AND FIND THE THING THAT MADE US FEEL BETTER BEFORE AND IT WILL JUST SEEM LIKE IT TAKES OVER - AGAINST OUR CONSCIOUS WILL... AND WE DO THE THING.

4

What Are We Really Addicted to?

> *Addictions begin with pain and end with pain.*
> *- Eckhart Tolle*

When we think of an addict, we may think of someone drunk, holding a bottle in a paper bag, or a heroin addict passed out in an alleyway with a syringe in their arm.

But addiction comes in all different forms. The main thing to know and be aware of is that addiction itself is the addiction to a *feeling,* even if it holds detrimental effects on our lives and others. For example, we might feel an emptiness inside, so we fill it with casual relationships, excessive spending or even constantly eating unhealthily. These are all acceptable in modest amounts, but when it starts to become one of our biggest drivers - to the point it takes away or is detrimental to other parts of our lives, then it is most likely an addiction or unhealthy coping mechanism.

When these occur, we tend to neglect or sacrifice other areas of our lives in order to fulfil the addictive behaviour, to obtain the feeling we get from it. We prioritise it, even if we don't admit it consciously. The issues start to add up, which over time can cause more stress and more reasons for us to need something to escape with, to cope with the effects of those decisions. As you can imagine, this creates a snowball effect and it's hard to break the cycle.

Having suffered from addictions myself, and, if you were to speak to someone with an active addiction, they most likely know of issues in other aspects of their lives or have already burnt a lot of bridges, but they will often still prioritise creating their life around it. But, whether consciously or unconsciously, the positive feelings must psychologically and physiologically almost always outweigh the negatives.
Excuses will be inevitable. Even when we hit rock bottom and decide we don't want to do it anymore, more often than not, if the underlying causes are not addressed through questioning, therapy, trauma healing and their lifestyle dramatically changing (letting go of toxic friends, relationships and ties to the addiction), then the need for an excuse will ensue and the addiction or *replacement addictions* will most likely continue again in some way.

Again, what we are actually addicted to is the feeling we get, and this is the number-one driver. Feeling good or good enough, feeling high, feeling peaceful, feeling love, feeling confident, feeling worthy, feeling accomplished and proud of oneself. If we cannot obtain that feeling naturally and if we can't meet the most ridiculous standards that society and advertising set, then we seek that same feeling through other means. And when we find what works for us, our brain certainly remembers and reminds us. Some people are more addicted to the feeling of completing goals, some are addicted to trying to find the feeling of being loved through opioids or relaxation through depressants. So, when we find the vice of choice like over-working, drinking, excessive shopping, binge eating or drugs, then we have found a way to reward ourselves without having to achieve our life goals and we can relieve the stress we don't know how to release from our body, creating an escape.

What we don't realise is that when we are inspired by or jealous of someone else's success, it's not the success itself. It's not material goods, homes, and outfits, but it's the actual dedication, hard work and vulnerability to put themselves or their work out there. We admire their effort and their air of confidence, that they have believed in themselves. We admire courage when people push themselves out of their comfort zones.

Or we may look at someone with a lot of savings and wealth - and we may wonder, how do they delay gratification? If they received $100,000 two years ago, how did they refrain from spending it on partying and instead put it away in a high-savings account or invest it, quadrupling the amount?

Some of you might laugh at them for not enjoying it in the now - that's your ego, your shame. It's the part of you that justifies and makes the detrimental thing you're doing 'cool', so you can cope with the actual shame that you have around your addiction's grip on you.

This is felt and true on a soul level, and you may not have recognised this until right now. Next time you feel inspired by or jealous of someone - be aware of it, and then dig a little deeper. Be honest with yourself and see if you are actually inspired by their courage or if they are triggering your insecurities and shame of whatever it is that has a grip on you. Once you recognise this you will be able to see what is yet to be found inside you and use it as a launch pad to set yourself free.

I'll give you a personal example:

SINCE BEING IN A RELATIONSHIP WITH RYAN AND HAVING TOMMY, MY WEIGHT HAS GONE UP AND DOWN. I KNEW IT COULD TAKE SOME TIME TO LOSE WEIGHT AFTER HAVING A BABY. I BREASTFED SO USUALLY IT'S EASIER TO LOSE THE WEIGHT, AND I DID, INITIALLY. BUT SINCE THEN, IT HAD CONTINUED TO GO UP

AND DOWN. I KNEW I WAS TIRED AND STRESSED, AND THAT COULD CAUSE ME TO GAIN WEIGHT. IT WAS JUST ANOTHER EXCUSE I TOLD MYSELF, I GUESS. I WOULD OFTEN GOOGLE TO SEE WHAT IT COULD BE ATTRIBUTED TO. I KNEW MY BODY WAS NATURALLY SLIM, SO I REALLY COULDN'T WORK OUT WHY I WAS

SABOTAGING AND EATING SO MANY 'SNACKS' ALL THE TIME.

BECAUSE I COULDN'T WORK IT OUT, THE EGO STEPPED IN TO PROTECT ME. I COULDN'T BE WITH THE SHAME ON MY OWN, SO I WOULD START TO JUSTIFY

1. *"I STILL LOOK KIND OF SKINNY WITH CLOTHES ON", "I HAVE A FAST METABOLISM, SO I CAN LOSE WEIGHT WHENEVER I WANT",*

"RYAN DOESN'T MIND HOW I LOOK, HE STILL LOVES ME AND NEVER SAYS ANYTHING ABOUT MY WEIGHT, MAYBE HE DOESN'T NOTICE?", "I NEED LOTS OF

CALORIES BECAUSE I AM NURSING" ETC, ETC. BUT THEN, WITH SELF-AWARENESS, I REALISED THAT I WOULD FEEL JEALOUS

OF WOMEN WHO LOOK SKINNY AND FIT. I COULD SENSE A PART OF ME LONGING TO FEEL AND LOOK HEALTHY AGAIN AND BE ABLE TO WEAR WHATEVER CLOTHES I LIKED. I DIDN'T LIKE LOOKING AT PEOPLE JUDGMENTALLY... I DIDN'T WANT TO DO IT. BUT A PART OF ME WAS, AND IT WAS REALLY JUST ME JUDGING AND SHAMING MYSELF ON A DEEPER LEVEL WITH THE REFLECTION OF OTHERS. IT WAS WITH THAT AWARENESS THAT I HAD TO ADMIT THE FRUSTRATION AND START FINDING OUT WHAT WAS REALLY BEHIND MY SUGAR AND SNACKS

ADDICTION.

SO I TOOK MY OWN ADVICE AND BOOKED IN A SESSION FOR MYSELF. IN DELVING INTO THE DEEPER PARTS OF MY SUBCONSCIOUS MIND, WE FOUND MY BODY WAS JUST TAKING INSTRUCTIONS. BECAUSE OF MY PAST PROMISCUITY (AND THE SHAME I STILL HELD AROUND IT), I WAS SUBCONSCIOUSLY PROTECTING MY RELATIONSHIP WITH RYAN BY NOT BEING ATTRACTIVE TO OTHER MEN. A PART OF ME HADN'T RESOLVED THE SHAME THAT I HAD AROUND CHEATING ON A PREVIOUS PARTNER, AND IT WAS HELPING ME TRY TO AVOID THAT. AN OLD PART OF ME THOUGHT, 'IF I AM OVERWEIGHT THEN I

WON'T ATTRACT ATTENTION AND CHEAT AGAIN'. IT WAS AMAZING, ONCE THAT HAD SHIFTED, I FELT LIKE THE WEIGHT JUST AUTOMATICALLY STARTED MELTING OFF ME. MY SUGAR CRAVINGS LEFT IMMEDIATELY. THE SNACKING JUST STOPPED!

HAVE A SABOTAGE THAT YOU WOULD LIKE TO WORK ON AND ARE INTERESTED IN A HEALING SESSION YOURSELF? VISIT OUR PRACTITIONER DIRECTORY AT

WWW.THECENTREFORHEALING.COM/PRACTITIONER-DIRECTORY

So what is in the way of us believing in ourselves and finding the courage to complete long-term goals or pursuits?

I believe it's our society's addiction to comfort and instant gratification.

These days, we instantly get a response from someone on our phones, we warm up food within minutes, we have on-demand movies and if we are feeling warm, we can put the air conditioner on and be cooled down quickly. We live in an age of comfort (in western society, anyway). With all of these conveniences, we have now been cursed with expecting everything now and not having to work too hard to have our basic needs met.

Instant gratification is what is essentially blocking us from going through the challenges of growing towards what we want to accomplish or bring to the world in this life. Dopamine (which motivates us) is released when we grow through challenges, and then there's a larger hit when we accomplish something. Another issue most of us have is the lack of nurture from a young age to *do what we want*. It was often leaning towards what would make our parents happy. You can see the younger X and Y generations realising this, putting the brakes on and resisting being told what to do, because they can see how miserable most of us are.

After doing this for a while, we get despondent and think: "What is the point? I got the car I've always wanted, got the job my parents pushed me to get and spent all my spare money to look good to my friends, but I am still not happy".

If you are reading this and you feel you haven't achieved the above, or what society classes as 'making it', then what I have talked about might not resonate with you. Maybe you are someone who has never achieved anything, you feel like you're just floating around, just trying to get by each day. Maybe you feel like you are the disappointment of the family - and always feel as though people look down on you, feel sorry for you and think you are lazy. But there is no right or wrong way to live your life - just *your* way. Feeling safe and accepted is all that matters in the end.

I came to this realisation myself after the following experience. At the time of writing this, my father had passed away only a few months earlier. My dear father Fred, to who I have dedicated this book. I felt I needed to speak to him on the other side. I have no doubt there is another side, but I kept an open mind and didn't expect too much when I booked a medium to allow a channel for me to speak to him. I was completely blown away by the accuracy of what the reading was - from his mannerisms to his favourite cooler, to explaining both of my grandmothers accurately, as though I was really speaking to him.

He was born and raised in Germany over 85 years ago. He was taught from a young age that it was lazy to sit around and do nothing. He would sometimes make comments about my brother having something wrong with him because he hadn't done the usual socially acceptable route of finishing school etc. In the reading my father apologised to me for putting him down, understanding that his workaholic ways were not the only or right way. He said sorry for the comments, having processed this through healing as he went to the other side after his death, recognising that my brother grew up in a different, more relaxed home. It was a beautiful moment of forgiveness and realisation that you should just live your life your own way. We ended our amazing conversation with him saying to me "Bend like Willow", "as it's unbreakable with your hands and it's stronger to be flexible, just like that tree".

5

Trauma Bonding

> *I wanted my mother to love me. Despite all the torture and brutality.*
> *- Wendy Hoffman*

Relationships with others are normally a key part of our satisfaction in life. They seem to be able to make or break us and our happiness - if we allow them to. The bonds we create with others can come from healthy connections and common interests - or they can come from bonding over unconscious or subconscious unresolved trauma.

We tend to connect with people who have naturally familiar traits to us. Why? Perhaps because they reflect the traits we like about ourselves back to us, which then creates a natural likeness to them.

So why would we blindly get into negative relationships that can dull our joy, inner peace and natural high for life? Why don't we always choose the right people to be in company with, or put up with toxic relationships, workplaces, and romantic partners? Being human is not black and white. We are not all perfect, happy, or healthy 100% of the time. It would be easy to find negatives in anyone and become isolated and alone very quickly, missing out on the tapestry and variety of experiences in life.

So what do we need to look out for so we don't sabotage our own lives?

Trauma bonding. If you are wary enough to recognise this early on, then it could be a great tool for growth, expansion, and liberation for both parties involved.

How?

Firstly, let's go into what exactly trauma bonding is.

"Bonding is a biological and emotional process that makes people more important to each other over time. Unlike love, trust, or attraction, bonding is not something that can be lost. It is cumulative and only gets greater, never smaller. Bonding grows with spending time together, living together, eating together, making love together, having children together, and being together during stress or difficulty. Bad times bond people as strongly as good times, perhaps more so.

Bonding is, in part, why it is harder to leave an abusive relationship the longer it continues. Bonding makes it hard to enforce boundaries because it is much harder to keep away from people with whom we have bonded. In leaving a long relationship, it is not always useful to judge the correctness of the decision by how hard it is, because it will always be hard.

Moreover, experiencing extreme situations and feelings together tends to bond people in a special way. Trauma bonding, a term developed by Patrick Carnes, is the misuse of fear, excitement, sexual feelings and sexual physiology to entangle another person. Many primary aggressors tend toward extreme behaviour and risk-taking, and trauma bonding is a factor in their relationships.

Strangely, growing up in an unsafe home means later unsafe situations have more holding power. This has a biological basis beyond any cognitive learning. It is trauma in someone's history that makes for trauma bonding. Because trauma (and developmental trauma or early relational trauma is epidemic) causes numbing around many aspects of intimacy, traumatised people often respond positively to a dangerous person or situation because it makes them feel a rush. It is neither rational nor irrational. If survivors can come to see that part of the attraction is, while very unwanted, a natural process, they may be able to understand those feelings and manage the situation more intentionally."

- Excerpt: The Body Keeps the Score: Brain, Mind, and Body in the Healing of Trauma by Bessel van der Kolk MD.

As you can see, the patterns mentioned above can go on for lifetimes and generations and trick us into thinking we are happy and gaining small natural highs, but they are not true joy and they come from a place of unmet needs and trauma. They are temporary highs of the ego; the rush, the false high.

Once you recognise that you do this, you can start to heal and unravel and move forward into truly healthy relationships, which are not only joyful but also balanced and reciprocated.

Here is a personal example:

MY PARENTS SEPARATED WHEN I WAS ABOUT 3 YEARS OLD. MY FATHER WAS A LOVELY MAN (DESPITE HIS ALCOHOL BINGES ON THE WEEKENDS). HE WAS KIND AND ATTENTIVE. MY MUM WAS YOUNG AND INNOCENT BUT SHE DECIDED TO LEAVE MY DAD DUE TO THE MANY CULTURAL DIFFERENCES THEY HAD. AS I WAS GROWING UP, MY MUM CONTINUED TO DATE PEOPLE WHO HAD ADDICTIONS AND WERE SOMEWHAT ABUSIVE. THE MAIN ONE WAS MY STEPDAD FOR AROUND SIX YEARS. HE WAS AN ALCOHOLIC AND PHYSICALLY ABUSIVE TOWARDS MY MUM AND WOULD HIT HER IN FRONT OF MYSELF AND MY BABY BROTHER AND SISTER. WHEN I STARTED DATING, I HAD A FEW PARTNERS WHO WERE VERY LOVING AND CARING, BUT BECAUSE OF THE STRESS I ENDURED IN THE ENVIRONMENT GROWING UP, IT WAS ALMOST LIKE I FELT UNCOMFORTABLE IN THOSE RELATIONSHIPS. I WOULD SABOTAGE THEM

BECAUSE I DIDN'T FEEL THE RUSH, AND A PEACEFUL AND LOVING RELATIONSHIP WAS A FOREIGN FEELING FOR ME. I THEN MET SOMEONE WHO HAD SO MANY SIMILAR TRAITS TO MY ABUSIVE STEPDAD THAT IT WAS UNCANNY - BUT I DIDN'T SEE IT AT THE TIME. I HAD NO AWARENESS OF THE MAGNETISM THAT OCCURS ON AN UNCONSCIOUS LEVEL WHEN YOU HAVE UNRESOLVED TRAUMA. I MISTOOK THIS MAGNETISM FOR CHEMISTRY AND ATTRACTION. I RUSHED INTO THAT RELATIONSHIP. DESPITE ALL THE RED FLAGS AND DISAPPROVAL FROM PEOPLE WHO CARED ABOUT ME. DESPITE THE CONTROL, EMOTIONAL ABUSE AND ADDICTIONS, I STAYED. THEN LEFT, AND THEN WENT BACK (A COMMON THEME WHEN IT

COMES TO DOMESTIC VIOLENCE VICTIMS THAT MANY PEOPLE DON'T

UNDERSTAND). IT WASN'T UNTIL I WAS INSPIRED BY SOMEONE ELSE THAT I HAD THE COURAGE

AND LEFT AGAIN. BUT THIS TIME WAS DIFFERENT. THIS TIME I STARTED WORKING ON MYSELF, STARTING WITH PERSONAL DEVELOPMENT AND THEN

DELVING INTO THERAPY AND HEALING. NOW I AM WITH THE MOST AMAZING MAN IN A PEACEFUL AND HAPPY

RELATIONSHIP. SOMETIMES I HAVE AWARENESS BROUGHT TO ME ABOUT MORE BAGGAGE THAT

NEEDS TO BE HEALED FROM THE PAST, WHEN I EXPECT TO BE ATTACKED OR IGNORED AND MY

NERVOUS SYSTEM REACTS IN FEAR. BUT I AM NOW FREE TO TALK ABOUT ANYTHING THAT I AM THINKING ABOUT IN THIS RELATIONSHIP. I

AM FREE TO BE WHO I AM AND HAVE THE SPACE TO GROW. I AM GRATEFUL TO SAY THAT I FINALLY FEEL SAFE TO BE LOVED.

M.K HIEMANN

6

Just Coping

> *All the contortions we go through are just not to be ourselves for a few hours -Keith Richards*

Coping mechanisms serve as a way and are an effort to try to feel good when your baseline or natural state of feeling is very negative, and it creates an inability to be able to sit with yourself peacefully.

People can have many coping mechanisms they're unaware of and that could be unconsciously running their lives. Sadly, most western and modern psychology actually teaches people coping mechanisms in order to be able to move forward in life, rather than looking at what they are coping with and why.

For example, a coping mechanism could be to go and punch a punching bag or go to the gym if you're feeling angry. Advice like this might be helpful, but like treating symptoms only, it will have to be implemented over and over again because it's not treating the root cause. Another way to look at it is like it's a band-aid that will need to be reapplied as soon as it wears off. To realise the natural high, we need to let go of the coping mechanisms, and more importantly, actually, heal and release what we are coping with.

Running an addiction and mental health clinic for many years has given us great insight into what people are coping with and why. As humans, we are so complex and have so many layers and patterns that make up who we are, that it would be an injustice to generalise coping behaviours with general issues that are happening in our lives, in the now.

When a client comes in, we observe and associate coping mechanisms in terms of energy. If we assume there is a baseline energy of inner bliss or peace that we can perhaps feel deep down or remember we have, every degree, decision, relationship, and purchase is all in an effort to feel this 'inner peace'. Anything below this line is perceived as a negative emotion and anything above the line is seen and felt as a positive or happy emotion.

How can we then diagnose or assist someone through an examination of their energy level? Our energy level, on a physical level, is the window into what is happening biochemically and mentally. Take ice addiction or methamphetamine substance abuse. This substance is known as a stimulant. It gives a huge release of energy that can last for days at a time - so much so that the user does not even require sleep. What is it that is giving all this energy? Energy only comes from within - externally we can only try to manipulate the chemicals and resources that are already inside our bodies by ingesting them. What it does is release a huge amount of the chemical dopamine. When I say release, I mean it blocks or inhibits the reuptake or recycling of dopamine - so huge amounts of it are set free in the brain. Dopamine is the chemical that gives us the energy to go through challenges, to work through and achieve our goals, and most importantly will give us a huge feeling of reward. Unfortunately with ice, this is a false high and the user could feel like they are achieving big goals, when they may just be moving rubbish from one side of the house to the other. But why is it that some people get addicted and some people don't? From our personal experience conducting thousands of addiction recovery sessions, it's all an energy game and a need for the attainment of a natural high.

From experience, we find the heavier the emotions someone has bottled up and carries as baggage, like shame, guilt, depression, and apathy (often since childhood) - the better and more tempting the instant false high is, and therefore the easier it is to become addicted. If someone is already working towards or living their ideal life and they don't have the ongoing aggression of inner negative self-talk, then their dopamine levels are already working normally.

Due to their baseline being higher, it actually makes them feel too highly strung, so they decide not to continue using.

There are a few key indicators that can determine whether you are spending a lot of time just coping or not. Here are some questions to ask yourself:

Do you find it uncomfortable to sit in silence? For example, do you always have to have the music on in the car, or the TV on at home?

Do you always have to have something in your hands or mouth? Like constantly doing - cleaning, eating, smoking, or fidgeting?

Can you spend long periods of time by yourself without communicating by phone or online to someone, or do you always feel like you want to reach out to people as you feel uncomfortable being alone?

Do you find you always need alcohol or other substances before and while socialising with others?

Do you neglect yourself when it comes to your health and other areas of your life in order to focus on helping others with their problems rather than your own?

Do you overly care about what other people think of you and beat yourself up when you don't get the validation from them that you desire?

Do you find yourself reaching for unhealthy snacks when you are emotional?

Do you try to pressure others to use substances with you, so you feel less ashamed of yourself?

If you find yourself answering yes to the majority of the above, then it is highly likely that you are under emotional and mental stress and overwhelm, which is impacting the way you look after yourself, and it may be blocking you from feeling purposeful and happy. Don't fret about these results too much, the majority of people have at least some of the coping mechanisms mentioned above, simply because life isn't always easy, and we are just trying to do our best and get by the best way we know how.

Instead of thinking that you are now burdened with the self-abuse as mentioned above, as a way to cope with what has happened to you, look at these indicators as an opportunity to delve deeper - knowing that with each layer healed, these compulsions will start to subside naturally and easily (where willpower only lasts so long).

How much torture do many people go through in stopping soothing themselves, but forever thinking about it for the rest of their lives... addiction should not be a battle, it should be an invitation to go within and start to set ourselves free.

M.K HIEMANN

7

Labels: The Life Sentence

> *Ignore those who say just get over it. Healing is a process. - HealthyPlace.com*

Unfortunately, many people hold grudges from childhood or their first love, always blaming and still bitter many years later. Forever heartbroken and either depressed and scraping by or outwardly angry and bitter towards people and the world because of the pain they still feel. If this is you, you will be feeling angry and hurt reading this. If this is someone you know then they will be coming up in your mind.

They relied on the person, clothes, job title or car to show their worth. But the moment it is taken away or they lose the things that propped up their ego for a while, they feel worthless and blame everyone else. Yes, it may have been someone else's fault, but they can decide whether it is a life sentence or not.

As in, will they take some responsibility, learn from it, perhaps become wiser and more humble and allow themselves to move on and move forward? Or will they stay locked behind the sentence of blaming the outside world and waiting for someone to save them, or for the world to notice they are in pain?

What we were told when we were children, things like "you are naughty", or when the mean kids at school called us overweight or ugly, or even the environment we were brought up in that made us feel unsafe in the world. These all factor into who we are now, depending on how much we believe them. Beliefs about ourselves or the world are generally created from ages 0-12.

Mistakenly, we think a lot of our behaviours - the way we talk and think - are just part of our personality that can never be changed. This has been disproven to us time and time again in our clinic. We can heal things that don't serve us - like sabotages, aggression, social anxiety, and negative habits that take our joy and bliss away or are roadblocks to the life we want. Then we can feel more balanced emotionally, do better things, and have more productive lives.

But some beliefs and 'life sentences' can be taken on as adults too. Particularly if we fully trust the person who is helping us create the negative belief. For example, a person who has had a sibling pass away in childhood - found it very difficult and didn't have the support to process the grief appropriately. Years later, this person suffers from depression and addictions - they find it very difficult to reach a natural high or inner peace, so they seek substances and sleep to cope with life. This person wonders if they should see a doctor and ask for help, hoping there may be an easy way out. Their doctor or psychiatrist asks them questions about their symptoms and diagnoses them with depression. Particularly in western society, doctors and the like are trusted. But instead of asking their patients about any trauma they are still dealing with and having a way to finally release and heal it, they label them, tell them they have a chemical imbalance and to take some more 'drugs' to suppress the emotions, in order to help them cope better. It is not their fault; they have such limited time and are restrained by what they are taught and allowed to deliver.

This is the issue with western medicine. It continuously treats the symptoms without treating the root cause. This manifests into many physical and mental issues later down the track. If people are falling victim to their emotions and then told they still don't have hope because their brain chemistry is not working properly and that "you just have to manage it for the rest of your life" - without guiding them to deal with the underlying cause, with no hope of overcoming it, just managing it...that sounds like a life sentence to me. Perhaps the doctor or psychiatrist gets to use you like a guinea pig to try different combinations of medications until one 'works' or suppresses how you feel sufficiently enough.

All the while, they enjoy the ongoing kickbacks by way of commissions from pharmaceutical companies. Where is the care and what century are we in? Thank goodness that western society is waking up to an empowered way of looking at health and going back to eastern philosophies to focus more on preventative and multidimensional care.

We aren't saying you should not seek help from your doctor or hospital. We are certainly advocating that you reach out for help in the easiest way you can to start the journey. There is a place for western medicine and doctors do an amazing job helping people with acute and urgent healthcare. We agree that medication is sometimes good for short-term emergency relief until the underlying causes can start to be addressed and dealt with. Ask anyone who is on medication - they probably don't like it and really don't want to take it. They intuitively know it's not right for their body because it's already constantly trying to balance itself out, and it's just another toxin that needs to be dealt with.

This does not come from opinion; this comes from evidence-informed methods and the witnessing of the many people we see in our clinics and who see other practitioners that work with the underlying causes. We see people completely shift and obtain not only homeostasis and balance, but also find joy, purpose and their natural high in life.

I myself, and through our team at The Centre for Healing, have personally seen
   hundreds of people overcome their mental health labels. Things from diagnoses of clinical depression to PTSD, anxiety and other labels. Many people turn to us, being an alternative health clinic

when they have tried different mainstream therapies and medications for years.

M.K HIEMANN

8

Clearing The Blocks

> *Imperfect action beats perfect inaction every time*
> – Harry Truman

Procrastination. The dream killer. You think to yourself - maybe for many years - when I get *[insert thing]* then I'll be happy. When I move to *[insert location]* I'll be happy. The reality is that your perfect car, partner, house, and life is pretty unlikely to fall into your lap. In fact, that doesn't even really matter anyway when it comes to *real* inner happiness. I have met very wealthy people who aren't content and are stressed out of their minds. They continue to drive themselves into the ground for fear of not being good enough or accepted by others. On the other end of the spectrum, we have met people that can't even get the energy to get out of bed in the morning. Or the middle ground of doing things they aren't really passionate about because they have anxiety and negative self-talk that continuously talks them out of their dreams. Shutting down and not listening to the inner voice that keeps telling them to do something they love, for fear of what people will think if they fail, or for not believing they are worthy. I have experienced both ends of the spectrum at different points in my life and have found a few key ways that can help to gauge where you are right now, in relation to where you want to be. To clear the walls in your mind, or your clients' minds, to achieve the best version in each moment, and continuously improve in different areas of your life.

Firstly, think about what you procrastinate about the most. Grab a piece of paper or go to the notes section in the back of this book and write them down.
Here is my list as an example to get you started:

For many years I had been wanting to paint. I would even go into an art shop if I saw one but would end up walking out empty-handed every time, talking myself out of it.
From age 22, I desperately wanted to start my own business. I had no idea what, I came up with an idea here or there and would do some research but then make up excuses and leave it for months and years on end.
I really enjoy nature and plants and wanted to bring them into my home. I had unfortunately killed a few plants in my past and disappointed myself, so I gave up and left it for a good six years.
These are just a few examples to get you thinking, but you can just list your dreams - they are often childhood dreams or inspirations. Most of you would know exactly what I am talking about; that little voice that has been in the back of your mind for years.

THE NATURAL HIGH

Note that what you have perhaps thought about might be weird in other people's eyes, but it is often helpful and life-affirming, no one can get hurt and all is in integrity. That's how you know you will obtain a natural high. Dreams that can negatively impact others will ultimately negatively impact you - so be clear on this and your intention (or the 'why'), behind your ideas.

Can you notice that all of the examples have a pattern? We can, for years and years, get flashes, callings, and reminders of our deepest inner dreams. But just as quickly as they come, we swiftly reply internally with excuses.

The root of the main excuses or deep internal blocks could be: I am not good enough
I am not worthy I fear being heard
I am not smart enough
I am scared it's not perfect
What people will think of me if I fail?

The hardest part is the blocks that come up and the negative inner self-talk, they are so automatic and familiar that we take them as absolute truth! Here's a tip - our thoughts are not us. They usually pop up from our past painful experiences to try and protect us from experiencing them again.

A part of us knows that it is not actually dangerous, but we find it easier to be comfortable than to be uncomfortable and choose not to put ourselves out there or grow until it becomes our new normal or baseline.

We so easily think we are just the way we are because of our bloodline, our nationality, our neighbourhood or school, and that we cannot change into those 'lucky' people who seem to be fearless and doing what they *really* want.

These are the subconscious and unconscious blocks that stop us from doing what our heart and soul and physical body would bliss out on.

I personally set out on a journey to see if I could push myself through the perceived limitations that I had allowed others to put on me and that I had put on myself. I was told things when I was a child, and because it was from adults and my mind was open, I took the comments as truth. Things like 'you would forget your head if it wasn't screwed on', or showing someone my artwork and them having the reaction of 'what a waste of art supplies'. When told things like this as a child, and if you accept this with a strong enough negative emotion, then it will most likely still be affecting you today.

I had a spark within me, but every time I wanted to move forward and take action, my mind would tell me reasons why I shouldn't. Only when your inner self-talk is stronger than other people's opinions of you will you actually be a driving force in your own life and be able to create whatever your heart desires, without the need for external validation.

Another common procrastination trap, or a delay on taking action on your dreams, is the need for comfort and security. Sure, it's a basic human need and in no way am I denying that.

THE NATURAL HIGH

But the issue is when this need for comfort overrides and creates a massive fear and aversion to any kind of challenge. Every single person on earth gets challenged in some way, but I believe a more empowered way is that we can *choose our challenges* rather than challenges choosing us.

So, when you feel like holding back on taking action, ask yourself - am I letting the fear of challenge override my pull towards my purpose or what I really want to do? Do I want to get to the end of my life, look back and think I didn't do anything *I* really wanted to do because I wanted to be comfortable, or I was afraid of other people's judgments - did I procrastinate instead of really living?

I understand people can get overwhelmed. There are so many internal obstacles that when we get to the external obstacles it's way too much and too hard - so we just give up. The best way to get through this is by baby steps. Taking little bites over time can accomplish much more than not even starting. Time passes anyway, so you may as well do a little bit every day (or every other day) to create momentum 'magic'. For example, if you save $2 a day - which isn't really noticeable to most people - in a year that can add up to $730!

When I was going through a hard time, the home I had worked hard for and the relationship I had, both crumbled before me. Externally I looked like I was doing very well - a sports car, an executive job, and a house by the beach. The truth is it felt like my body and soul were dying. I was anxious and couldn't wait for my next glass of wine or cigarette. The day I moved by myself into a one-bedroom rented apartment, I looked out the window at the ocean and felt so depressed and lost- I knew that something was very wrong. I also realised that if the people and external flashy things weren't helping me to achieve happiness, then all that was left was myself, and to face my inner self. I realised I could not escape myself anymore. No matter where I went, I was there.

This was a life-changing day.

It was the day I gave up trying to fight the world, or expecting everyone else to save me and fulfil my empty soul. At that moment, I finally broke through my tough ego that had been created over the years, and finally sought help. I finally got honest with myself. I had woken up at my rock bottom of depression; the accumulation of the terrible decisions I was making (or that the damaged parts of me were making). Interestingly, I later realised I had created this whole mess pretty much by myself, just involving and blaming others along the way. I was still in deep pain, in complete agony and was heartbroken. I still wanted to be the victim. Being the victim seemed easier; it made me feel like the right or good person, and then, the wrong and bad person. I waited for an apology so I could heal. I waited for someone else to make it right. It was initially hard to own up to, but to really heal and be back in control of and change my life, I had to take full responsibility for what had happened up until that point.

THE NATURAL HIGH

With the assistance of a therapist, who later became my trainer, we delved into my subconscious, where all of my life experiences from childhood had been held, and discovered defining moments that created my thoughts and behaviours which led me to where I was in my life at that point in time. Most of the beliefs that I made about myself and the world made me feel like I wasn't good enough, that I didn't love myself and I was desperately clinging to others to fill that gap, with a fake smile on my face. Not only that, I was still being affected by people that I was holding anger towards and hadn't forgiven from many years ago.

No wonder I was procrastinating on my inner desires - and it's why we all do to a degree. My inner self-talk and the heavy emotions I had accumulated over 26 years had taken over me and my dreams.

Once I started clearing those issues and realising a huge transformation in how I saw myself and the world, I studied how to become a therapist and healer and immediately went on the journey of opening my own coaching practice.

I was high on life, as I was finally answering my soul's dreams and felt higher than any drugs had ever taken me before. I took what I learned and continued to study human behaviour, psychology, spirituality, metaphysics, energy healing and shadow work, and relentlessly kept working on myself so I could help others and train people to be able to heal others so they could feel the natural high, too...

M.K HIEMANN

I NO LONGER NEEDED TO MOTIVATE MYSELF - I WAS BUZZING.

9

Healing Trauma

> *healing*
> *'hi:lɪŋ/ noun*
> *1. the process of making or becoming sound or healthy again.*

The hardest way to change is when people are telling you that you need to change. You know you are an amazing being, you just haven't found or tapped into how to express that yet. So, when someone tells you something negative, something that you are probably already internally telling yourself anyway, and especially if it's from someone close to you, it feels like a dagger stabbing through your heart.

You feel hurt, and the immediate emotional reaction can be to want to hurt them back or curl up in a ball and cry. The external world keeps confirming and giving you evidence. You berate yourself when you get a moment's silence, or you're faced with a challenge or choice. You know at some level they may be right, or it wouldn't hurt. But you are scared because you don't want to lose the connection and you don't know how to change - and you may have tried so hard before. You feel angry inside, your blood boils and you feel trapped in yourself. You can't stand the confirmation and ask yourself - how can I feel better and escape these terrible feelings and thoughts?

Your mind is a self-serving automated computer, quickly searching for the 'self-soothing' file and you automatically think about what has soothed you before. Getting smashed with your mates on alcohol, smoking a joint with an old friend, or bingeing on comfort food to temporarily swallow your feelings - even for a little while. Then in the aftermath, you often regret it and feel guilty because you know there is always a negative side effect of trying to lie and cheat yourself into some temporary happiness and instant gratification to escape. That then leads to feelings and thoughts of guilt and shame - "what's the point of me being here?

Why is life so hard? Why do I punish myself? I know it's bad for my health and bank account, why do I keep doing that?" Instant gratification turns into another thing to feel guilty about; another thing to be angry at yourself about; another confirmation of why you don't like yourself and why others were right in judging you. This is the cycle of guilt and shame and the cause of many addictions.

Life generally goes around in cycles. The seasons, the moon and tides, women's periods, watching our heartbeat on a monitor. So many other aspects go through ebbs and flows, and so do our life patterns. These can be like attracting the same kinds of friends, financial circumstances, and workplaces. Some of these life patterns - who and what we attract - can be positive and life-fulfilling, but some can be detrimental, painful, and frustrating.

These life patterns can lead to lethargy, apathy, depression, and frustration.

It's easy to blame the outside world and question "why does this keep happening to me?" It's easy to avoid making a strong decision and then get frustrated and angry, saying "this will never happen to me again!" Then we simply aren't going to be able get past it and will continue to play the victim. This is where healing comes into play and helps us break those life patterns that aren't serving us.

Healing doesn't mean the damage never existed. It means the damage no longer controls your life...
- Akshay Dubey

The first resistance that comes up when healing, and in particular healing, the trauma that started the life patterns, is "It wasn't my fault! They did this to me! I will never forgive them!"

It can often anger people, as it re-triggers the trauma and hurt they are still holding. This is a perfectly reasonable and normal reaction. The heartbreak, the divorce, the mistreatment or unfairness, either from recent times or from childhood. On the completely opposite end of the scale, people can wallow and not forgive themselves because "it was my fault, I deserved it".

I need to make it clear that it isn't actually about what they did in terms of right or wrong. The main thing about healing and forgiveness is to actually release the toxicity of resentment and pain from your mind and body; the heaviness from *your being*, so you can clear the space for your innocence, joy and awe for the world to return or be discovered.

The main part of our work in our healing centre was to hold hands with and help people in releasing this emotional pain - forgiving themselves and others. We have included a method that you can do at home if you are unable to find someone that can help with this kind of work, or you want to try it without going too deep.

I used this method with an old friend. She seemed to be struggling and I messaged her asking if I could help. She was a little sceptical about alternative methods as she was a registered nurse, but she seemed desperate and reached out for support. Her blood pressure was very high (190/100), and she really did not want to go to the hospital - she was willing to try anything. From experience as a therapist over the years, I know that high blood pressure is linked to unexpressed anger. In fact, I find most physical ailments are rooted in deeper emotional baggage that is stuck in the body. I asked her what had created or triggered so much anger in her. She told me a good friend had just passed away, but they didn't have contact recently because his girlfriend blocked their friendship. This made her feel upset and hurt and was making it difficult to allow herself to grieve.

I knew though, based on her blood pressure, that there was anger around this that she wasn't able to process and release, maybe due to the grief and shock. I told her to grab a piece of paper and write down how she was feeling. She wrote down some negative emotions and sent me a picture. It really wasn't what I meant so I had to ask her again, gently, to write out her thoughts emotionally. Like *why* did he kill himself? And *why* did his girlfriend keep him away from me? And who or what am I really upset with? I told her to keep writing until she couldn't write anymore, turning up whatever emotions were coming up, without filtering anything. I didn't hear from her for the next 10 minutes and then she sent me through what looked like aggressively written paragraphs on a lined A4 page. It was perfect.

I then told her to reassess her blood pressure, 150/70 - pretty much normal. She couldn't believe it. She thought she would need Valium or some other kind of medication and hospitalisation to get it down. She ended the chat conversation with "Thanks so much, Mel. I feel heaps better. Honestly".

The way to your spirit is through your body.

- Ashley Asti

Unfortunately, I never got the chance to do a deeper healing with her to see if this event had triggered some other painful experiences or traumas in her life (most likely due to her very highly charged emotional state).

So often we get asked, what is trauma exactly? As a part of experiencing life (not just from things like a car accident or sexual abuse), we all have our own perceptions and filters. We innately know what is right or wrong (from even around four months old in the womb). Imagine this, we come into this life, fairly whole and well. I like to use the mirror as an analogy for this. When we enter this world, we are somewhat of an oval-shaped mirror, with a little bit of wear and tear may be from ancestral or past life trauma, but pretty together.

When we see or experience something traumatic, in order to get on with ourselves and not be continually traumatised by the memory and feelings in our mind, a part of that mirror must break off. The gap that is caused is almost like a black hole or vacuum. But it still allows us to get on with our lives. Our mirror does want to mend, as do our bodies - just like when we have a physical wound, it tries its best to heal and come back into balance. How do you know if you have experienced major trauma? When that mirror breaks, it causes the image, the emotions, to disassociate. This may cause us to create what is called PTSD (post-traumatic stress disorder), and if this part of us is still trying to integrate and heal, we can have panic attacks from seemingly normal situations and people. It could appear as flashbacks when say, doing unconscious things like having a shower or driving. Because there is a lingering fear and we don't know why we can seek to numb it out with various mood-altering substances and behaviours. We are subconsciously attracted to people who have similar behaviours to the ones that originally caused the trauma. We ignore all the red flags in a desperate bid to try to recreate and finally heal that part of the mirror or, essentially, the break in our soul or heart.

We go through many traumas just as a result of growing up in our current society. These seemingly big or small traumas create patterns - life patterns, in fact. A good way to know if you have a recurring life pattern that needs to be healed is to notice when you frustratedly say "why does this always happen to me?"
It is the break in the mirror, desperately trying to be healed, unconsciously attracting the same circumstances like a magnet.

HERE IS A PERSONAL EXAMPLE OF MINE. I NEVER GOT ALONG WITH MY STEP-MUM. I KNOW THAT STEP-FAMILIES ARE NOT EASY AND CAN BE DIFFICULT TO NAVIGATE IN GENERAL. MY PARENTS SEPARATED WHEN I WAS AROUND 3 AND MY FATHER MET MY STEP-MUM NOT LONG AFTER THAT. THESE ARE IMPRESSIONABLE YEARS. ANYWAY, WHEN I WAS AROUND 7 YEARS OLD, I REMEMBER TELLING MY MUM THAT I DID NOT WANT TO GO TO MY DAD'S ANYMORE BECAUSE MY STEPMUM WAS A 'BITCH'. I REMEMBER MY FATHER COMING AROUND TO TALK TO ME ABOUT IT - AS WE WERE VERY CLOSE.

HE WAS UPSET WHEN I TOLD HIM AND I BELIEVE HE HAD A FEW WORDS WITH HIS PARTNER ABOUT WHAT I HAD SAID. SHE SEEMED TO BE NICE FOR A WHILE, BUT THAT WORE OFF (AS IT DOES WHEN YOU ARE PUTTING

ON A FACADE). FOR YEARS I WOULD WITNESS MY STEP-MUM SCREAMING AT AND TRYING TO CONTROL MY FATHER, EVEN IN HIS DECLINE WITH ALZHEIMER'S DISEASE. HE WOULD LOOK AT ME AND TRY AND MAKE IT A JOKE SO IT WOULDN'T IMPACT

ME SO MUCH. AWARE THAT SHE WAS STRUGGLING, AND PROBABLY UNKNOWINGLY BATTLING HER OWN INNER DEMONS, I TRIED TO IGNORE IT AND CONTINUED TO VISIT THEM. AS I WENT INTO ADULTHOOD, STARTED IN THE WORKFORCE AND LATER HAD MY

OWN BUSINESS - I NOTICED THAT I CONTINUED TO ATTRACT STRONG, ANGRY AND CONTROLLING WOMEN. WHETHER IT WAS CO-WORKERS, FRIENDS,

HOUSEMATES ETC. ALREADY ON THE JOURNEY, AND GETTING TIRED OF ATTRACTING THESE 'SAME PEOPLE, DIFFERENT FACE' SCENARIOS, INSTEAD OF BEING A VICTIM I SET OUT

ON A HEALING PATH TO FIND OUT WHY I WAS ATTRACTING THESE PEOPLE - WHAT WAS IT CALLING ME TO AWAKEN AND REALISE IN MYSELF?

IN LATER HEALING I HAD A REALISATION OF TWO WAYS THAT IMPACTED WHAT I ATTRACTED AND MY BEHAVIOURS IN RELATIONSHIPS:

- AS MENTIONED, I KEPT ATTRACTING THESE WOMEN INTO MY LIFE. EVEN WITH RED FLAGS I, FOR SOME REASON, FELT DRAWN TO THESE PEOPLE, OBVIOUSLY AN EFFORT TO REPLAY, ROLE-PLAY AND HEAL SOMETHING ON A

DEEPER LEVEL FROM MY UNRESOLVED CHILDHOOD TRAUMAS. 2. WHEN YOU ARE JUDGING SOMEONE FOR BEING A CERTAIN WAY, IT IS VERY LIKELY, ESPECIALLY IF THEY ARE IN A PARENT OR AUTHORITATIVE ROLE - TO

UNCONSCIOUSLY TAKE ON THOSE CHARACTERISTICS TO KEEP YOURSELF SAFE

BY BEING 'LIKE' THE ABUSER. I WAS LITERALLY EXPRESSING THESE BEHAVIOURS IN MY RELATIONSHIPS, RE-

ENACTING WHAT I SAW WITH MY FATHER AND STEP-MUM AND THEIR DYNAMIC

- RECREATING IT AGAIN IN AN EFFORT TO HEAL. IT'S VERY HARD FOR PEOPLE TO ADMIT THEY HAVE TAKEN ON TRAITS OF THEIR

ABUSERS AND IT'S OFTEN VERY UNCONSCIOUS OF OUR AWARENESS. OF COURSE, OTHER PEOPLE NOTICE, BUT IF THEY BRING IT TO OUR ATTENTION WE CAN BECOME EXTREMELY DEFENSIVE AND REACTIVE - THAT'S HOW YOU KNOW

A WOUND HAS BEEN HIT. LISTEN TO THEM AS THEY MAY BE TRUE.

M.K HIEMANN

THE NATURAL HIGH

10

Follow

> *Follow your bliss and the universe will open doors for you where there were only walls.*
> *- Joseph Campbell*

Have you ever heard the term "follow your bliss"? It's a well-meaning phrase! Believe it or not, this is, in some cases, actually a potentially dangerous quote. Whether it is dangerous or not highly depends on the person receiving it, how they were brought up, their life experiences and how they handle emotional and physical stress.

For example, if you say this to a person who struggles immensely with overwhelming depression, or flashbacks from the trauma inflicted on them or by them onto others, if they have already been exposed to the numbing and mind-altering effects of drugs, addictions and medications - then they will use these. That is their association with 'bliss' because they have yet to find another way. And this could be to the detriment of other areas of their lives, to avoid sitting in the pain of their negative emotions and thoughts.

If you say the same thing to someone who has had a supportive life or has taken the time to work on their personal development, then saying this to them can be beneficial as they are not dealing with a great amount of pain to escape, and it will likely manifest as working towards challenges and growth to achieve goals that give them positive energy and guided intuition.

Although following your bliss is a major key to the *natural high* - we must be able to discern between healthy and unhealthy forms of bliss before blindly taking this instruction. Asking questions to check the ecology, like: "Will this negatively affect my body, finances, my future self or emotions later on? Will it negatively affect anyone else around me? Is it something I want to hide away and would be ashamed to tell anyone else about? Am I respecting myself and my values?"

Instant gratification can literally sabotage our future selves and plans. Delayed gratification and enjoying the journey (whether it be challenging or not) will generally always pay off. Bursts of bliss come from holding off or feeling challenged now, rather than delaying it and letting it accumulate, or even just as simple as resting today so we have energy for tomorrow.

For example, the ego or our shadow self is literally in the shadows. It has been buried to save us from some of the pain and protects us so we can move forward somewhat. If you often say, "I don't know why I do that?", this is frequently an indicator of a program running on a deeper level, which is creating and getting benefits from something that could be sabotaging us. This sneaky part of us will present thoughts as excuses. For instance, with my clients who want to shift behavioural or substance abuse issues, something I ask them in order to help monitor their progress and help them overcome issues is, what are the excuses which pop up into your mind when you go to do [*insert vice of choice here*].

Here are some common examples of these thoughts:

- "Smoking helps me relax"
- "I need to eat when I am bored"
- "I deserve this drink"
- "I need this to feel better"
- "I need it to sleep"

These are surface-level thoughts that come up into our awareness and, if we are not mindful, they literally tell our bodies what to do. Even if you consciously don't want to do it, it is like your body takes on a mind of its own and all of a sudden you have a wine in hand without even thinking about it.

So what are the thoughts behind the thoughts? The drivers? The subconscious and unconscious payoffs?

Our body is hardwired to keep us in balance. A state of relaxation and homeostasis. If we are not in this state, it will automatically draw on past experiences of how it got there, within milliseconds you are doing or thinking about how to get out of the current state of stress or emotional uncomfortableness. Willpower only lasts so long. This is a relapse.

So to overcome this, what can we do? How do we stop just thinking about ourselves? How do we start releasing this stress from our bodies, so we don't have to manipulate trying to find peace with things that negatively affect us and those around us?

This is what my life's work now is all about. The creation of our healing centre, the creation of our method Root-Cause Therapy, it's all about releasing the underlying reasons why.

I invite you to access our free course to discover how Root-Cause Therapy works and request to see a demonstration session at https://www.thecentreforhealing.com/webinar-registration

M.K HIEMANN

THE NATURAL HIGH

11

The Ripple Effect

> *Having a healing business is not just about you, it's about healing the world and being of service to your soul's mission - Melissa Hiemann*

Have you ever seen an object being thrown into still water? If so, you would have seen the ripples it creates. As the rays or reverberations go out from the point of creation and contact, the effect gets larger and wider in size to the outer corners of the container or body of water. This also happens energetically in ways on a human-to-human level.

Our ego or mind can say: "my life is pretty good; I'm doing pretty well compared to this person who has it worse off than me or is grumpier than me". Yes, you might be doing slightly better in your outer world, but how do you know that you are actually doing better, or that you are a happier person? We are so complex and all experience life so different in so many ways that a) making assumptions can be very inaccurate and b) comparing ourselves to others is a sure way to never find inner happiness.

We often have people come into our healing clinic wanting advice on how to change someone else, blaming them for their stress and unhappiness. It is true that others' negativity can directly affect our lives. But if we leave it up to others to change, believing that it will resolve our happiness, then we will always rely on others and be at the whim of their actions or inactions. The truest and best way that you can bring peace and happiness to your life is to take full responsibility. This could include learning and understanding yourself so you can grow and improve your relationship with yourself. Or it could be creating financial and emotional boundaries so you can fill your cup and be a more caring person when you are called to help someone or the world. It could include following a passion that you haven't allowed yourself to yet - particularly if you are frustrated that the other person isn't focusing on improving. The general pattern is not being contradictory and practising what you preach. Also know you can't always save people.

Everyone has their own journey - *whether you agree with it or not.*

We can't just expect others to change so that *we* can feel better. That's unfair. Imagine for yourself, constantly being told you're not good enough, that your actions are not good enough and you need to change. No one likes that deep down. Instead, we can look at our relationships for the purpose they were intended - to experience this thing called life, and challenge and support each other along the way.

One theory that I often hear in the spiritual community is that our experience of life is the universe's attempt to meet and experience itself. If we then go back to the mirror analogy of the soul, imagine each of us as a mirror fragment of the universe having a relationship with itself. Every time we judge someone, it's just a reflection of what we judge in ourselves that we are not aware of yet. Or every time we like someone, they are just reflecting the parts of us that we already admire in ourselves and so we 'like' them.

Imagine how much more empowered you would feel if every time something triggered you, cut you deeply, you looked within yourself rather than attacked the outside world. Then you are no longer a victim to your life, but rather your own saviour and generally probably a great person to be around.

A great way to understand this is to try the following next time you find yourself judging someone.
Example:
"That person is really negative and toxic," you say with a frown on your face. When you notice yourself doing it, immediately turn the phrase towards yourself, such as "I am a really negative, toxic person".
Notice how at that moment you were actually being a negative, toxic person, by your judgment!

Try doing this every time you go to judge someone or think someone *should* or *shouldn't* be doing something, and watch your judgments start to reduce over time. Judgments are really a key to shining the light on our blind spots or behaviours that we are unconscious to and need to change in ourselves.

If we then look at this from a healing perspective, and the potential of what healing just one person at a time can have on collective humanity, isn't it worth going on the journey? Isn't it worth diving into the pain of our triggers so we can transmute it to inner peace? Isn't it worth facing our demons so we can have a more relaxed and free life?

Forgiveness doesn't mean what they did to us was right in any way, its purpose is to set ourselves free from the emotional pain and physical issues that may be occurring by holding onto the hurt, so it's no longer a burden on our lives.

Every single person affects the whole. Each person that is healing or on the personal development journey positively affects the whole. Each parent that decides they will be a conscious and aware parent and be trauma-informed, creates a whole new generation of grounded adults interacting together, influencing how we look after the planet and each other in a more positive way.

Every time someone heals their anger on the road makes peace with the opposite sex and leads a more compassionate life - like the stone in the pond, it really does make a difference through each more peaceful interaction.

LOOK AT OTHERS LIKE THEY ARE A VERSION OF YOU,
   JUST LIVING A DIFFERENT LIFE.

THE NATURAL HIGH

12

Bigger Issue

> *Everyone has been made for some particular work, and the desire for that work has been put in every heart .- Rumi*

We are consciously and unconsciously influenced by our family, friends, work colleagues, brands, and society in general. The degree to which they can influence you into either greatness or mediocrity is based on how aware you are of the influence, and to what degree you will allow it (or them) to influence your decisions, actions, and goals. Depression is becoming so prevalent, particularly in western society, that even though our quality of living and health services are improving, somehow, we are getting unhappier over time. Especially in western societies, happiness is valued over experiencing or showing any negative emotions. Suppress your negative emotions over time and mental illnesses are inevitable.

THE NATURAL HIGH

Why is there depression or unhappiness despite having almost everything we need at our fingertips and having our basic needs met? Well, it is most likely the expectations impressed upon us of how we should be, look and obtain; milestones to achieve based on *other* people's ideas, values, and goals. A lot of people find they reach a point where they achieve standard goals but still aren't fulfilled internally, questioning all the years and work put in towards achieving what seems to be a fleeting moment of happiness. Depression is therefore a combination of living to impress others around us based on society's marketing
and rules, and finding we want to resist it as we notice over time that it is not aligned with what we actually want. Then this can turn into anger at the unfairness of not getting what we want, like a toddler tantrum, and then turning this anger towards ourselves.

To explain further, there's an interesting example of the most successful businessmen or women, who are often people that didn't finish university. A billionaire study was completed by a company called WealthX which conducted a yearly census of billionaires, and only a third of them were found to have graduated from college.

I guess you could say they were somewhat rebels and didn't allow conformity to shape them and rob them of their creativity and drive. They opted for freedom rather than the mould that school and then work try to create to keep us in consumerism and debt. We are by no means saying that you need to create a large company to find fulfilment - again it's about creating a life that you love, that is for you, and doing what it is that you want.

I have looked in the mirror every morning and asked myself: 'If today were the last day of my life, would I want to do what I am about to do today?' And whenever the answer has been 'No' for too many days in a row, I know I need to change something. — Steve Jobs

What is it that you have always dreamed of since you were a child, which you either told yourself or a loved one said, "don't be silly" or "there is no money in that"? If we have all come here for a reason and it takes all kinds of skills, knowledge, services, people, and products to create a society - then why can't our unique dream be a thread in the fabric of those needs? If you do happen to find yourself in a place where you feel like your soul is dying, finding that you aren't happy and you're sick of living to other people's standards, then

it is time to call back your intuitive calling. It may not be clear. You may just get hints along the path until you realise. It may take days, weeks, or months of introspection and redirection. Eventually, you will get there, you will know, and your natural high will guide you.

It may not be easy in the interim, but it wasn't easy dragging it out and doing it the other way - so you really have nothing to lose!

13

Consciousness

> *No problem can be solved from the same level of consciousness that created it.* - Albert Einstein

If you can understand consciousness, you can understand reality. If you can understand reality, then you can better understand how to interact with it and be able to create a life that induces a more ideal feeling state. It isn't about control; it is more about understanding. The term consciousness can be defined as *the state or quality of awareness; or of being aware of an external object or something within oneself...*

Despite the difficulty in *definition*, many philosophers believe there is a broadly shared underlying intuition about what *consciousness* actually is.

The fact is, we experience our external world *internally*. We label objects, things, and people, based on what we know, past experiences, and how it makes us feel, or what it invokes internally through all of our senses. These layers of perception and experience filter our pure consciousness - which is the awareness that is recording and experiencing the thoughts and witnessing reality as it unfolds. In saying this, we have all experienced different kinds of realities through time, and these allow us to perceive now, the past and the future differently from each other.

Over time we can lose our awe of life. Of witnessing moments without labels. Free from so many worries, burdens, and thoughts - just like when we were young children - being curious without expectations.

So where does consciousness come into play when it comes to experiencing a natural high? Accumulation. Just like a compounding interest account with a bank, the more conscientious choices we make, the more they will build and accumulate and add up over time. But this can be either positive or negative accumulation. We obviously want to build interest *(positive flow)* rather than fees *(negative flow)* over time.

Let me give you an example to explain this concept further. Let's say you are someone that always seems to attract drama, whether in your family or workplace. This drama creates hurt, negativity, and rifts in relationships. Over time, not only have you burnt bridges, but you have also held onto an unforgiving judgment and hurt. When you enter into new relationships, you are hyper-conscious of those around you, of signs they may say something behind your back or cause trouble for you. Your layers or filters are active with this, and you consciously spend time and energy watching out for this based on your past experiences. Like a protection mechanism. Now, we can either be a victim of these filters, or we can become conscious of the pattern and realise (or own) that we are the lowest common denominator in these situations. Being conscious allows us to own what we may be attracting and that we may be creating these circumstances. This can be hard, yet liberating, as you start to pierce through filters that will allow you to start to see through others. Soul-to-soul awareness (or conscious awareness to conscious awareness) creates empathy, more positive choices, and a more harmonious way to interact with others. This then creates more positive experiences and an accumulation of better emotional states, more luck, and better opportunities over time.

Whatever you want to heal in others, you are being called to heal in yourself
- Melissa Hiemann

Achieving higher states of consciousness (feeling high and peaceful) can be obtained naturally without mind-altering drugs, which normally have some kind of negative side effect or counterbalance. And it doesn't have to always be through some kind of music or anything you need to do. Sometimes, it is actually something we don't do - or something that we just allow. Our pure awareness or consciousness is innately high, in awe and buzzing with life. Tapping into that or spending time tapping into it regularly will allow you to create space for more regular higher states, and a release from the layers which weigh us down.

Most of our negative feelings actually occur when we are resisting what is happening at the moment. The resistance to *'what is'* can cause a myriad of emotions such as anger, sadness, or stress. If we can simultaneously see the positive and negative in each moment instead, of the gift, then we are on the middle ground of gratitude and peacefulness.

But what about horrendous acts of torture and cruelty you may ask? How can we find a positive in that? You don't have to find the positive - but you do deserve to finally let go and forgive so it doesn't torture you anymore. To do that we must allow the emotions to complete their process, move through us and release so we can try and find some kind of learning or gift (even if it's not to ever treat anyone else like that) and move on with our lives as peacefully as we can.

If this is triggering some trauma for you, be sure to contact a professional to help you work through it.

M.K HIEMANN

THE NATURAL HIGH

14

Attainment

> *Anything is possible when you have inner peace.*
> *- Anonymous*

If you are reading this and enjoying it, you are potentially already getting a little naturally high. Or maybe some heavy stuff has come up for you due to realisations as you read about the possible sources of how we sabotage our best lives. Either way, learning something new about yourself or a concept significantly raises dopamine in your brain - similar to when you are experiencing and learning something new as a child - because on a basic primal level it increases our chances of survival from an evolutionary point of view.

Now that you have the background from the previous chapters, we can start to delve into how to obtain this natural high. How we can re-activate the natural yet centred 'buzz' that is already within us, our inner genius? It's just waiting for us to tap into it.

One of the key secrets to ongoing attainment of the natural high, delaying instant gratification and finding peace, is the difference between living a fulfilling, purposeful and joyful life versus feeling like life is a daily struggle and that life is not fair. It's like most people who are working 50 hours a week not doing what they love - so that they can get a few hours here and there of bliss and relief, eventually hitting a wall or plateau and blaming the world for their woes.

To obtain what we know we are intrinsically after and yearning for, we must learn about intrinsic versus extrinsic goals.

Intrinsic goals are created in our imagination and our soul, which we yearn to
manifest into physical reality. These are the goals that we feel like doing, that no one would have to ask us to do as we are motivated internally to do them. These are the things and insights we think about when we are working away for someone else's dreams but wish we could be doing them for ourselves instead. The voice that drops in, that quiet whisper from our soul that over time we get better at ignoring or internally talk ourselves out of. I often say to my clients that they already know their purpose - I can take them and show them the future, which will only confirm their own intuitive knowing that they have already received it since childhood. In order to allow this into your reality, to stop

limiting yourself and coming up with the million reasons why you cannot do it, we have to look at your main motivation.

Why? Because the thoughts that come up are usually:

- What if I try and I fail? What would my family, friends and loved ones think of me? *The feeling that arises can be fear of judgment or shame.*
- What if I cannot make a decent living from it? Would I lose my house, be able to pay for food and feed my pets and/or kids? *This can be from PTSD from past experiences of struggle and poverty.*
- I don't know enough about it and I am scared or sure that I am probably not good enough to do it. *This one is called Impostor Syndrome and it's very common, but we all have to start somewhere!*
- If only my parents/ex-partner helped me more, I could be doing what I love now. *This can come from co-dependency issues, or many feelings of not being supported enough in the past.*
- My peers/parents will mock me if I tell them what I really want to do, and I don't want to feel ashamed. *This can be from thinking outside of the box, which is usually the most successful idea!*

Extrinsic goals are those that we think will get approval from others. They are things that we feel like we *have* to do, rather than exactly what we really feel like doing with our lives. They are the goals that our parents wanted us to achieve, what we think will get the most admiration from the opposite sex (or same-sex), or what we think is the most admired by society. These kinds of goals are dangerous because feeling like you have accomplished something completely relies upon validation externally from others. It's like walking on a tightrope. On one hand, we can be balanced, feeling motivated and fulfilled temporarily - but one or more negative comments from people we are trying to gain admiration from can knock our ego off the rope and the damage can set us down a dark path because it cuts so deep. Think about movie stars or football players who stop getting public attention.

How many of those become addicted to drugs, chasing the feeling and high they previously got from others' admiration?

As the examples above show, it seems the intrinsic goals are the ones that are safely everlasting and can ensure the passion lives on. The courage and energy it takes to do what your soul desires actually attracts admiration, it's like a light and inspiration for others because they wish they could have the courage to do that too. External admiration comes as a side benefit of fulfilling intrinsic goals - *but is not reliant on external validation.*

Belief in yourself is more important than endless worries of what others think of you. Value yourself and others will value you. Validation is best that comes from within.
—— *Ngũgĩ wa Thiong'o, Dreams in a Time of War*

The natural high is no longer a fleeting buzz here and there. It takes us, it carries us through life's ups and downs and is an

anchor of safety within ourselves. It is our peaceful resilience. It doesn't knock other people over to get
what we want. It is always of integrity, conscious of self-love and not harming others, of making a positive impact on the world.

Our worth and value is no longer based on whether someone stays with us or not. because our worth is manifesting into the way we live and what we do, and most importantly what we create from our hearts.

POSITIVE EMOTIONS SHOULD BE FLEETING, NEGATIVE EMOTIONS SHOULD
BE FLEETING, PEACEFULNESS AND PRESENCE SHOULD BE THE BASELINE AND
GOAL.

THE NATURAL HIGH

15

Longevity

> *Sometimes the most productive thing you can do is relax.* –Mark Black

Now we've looked at attainment, let's look at how to ensure the longevity of the natural high. One of the keys to this is to listen to your body and allow yourself to tune into not only your biorhythms but your energy and motivation rhythms, too. To do this we must allow ourselves to relax sometimes. Countless times I have found my clients unconsciously holding the belief that *it is not OK or safe, or that it's lazy, to relax*. These people force and push themselves daily, using stimulants to keep going and depressants like wine to wind down at the end of the day. I was certainly one of those people too! This inevitably leads to burn-out, substance abuse and physical deterioration - all of which are detrimental to our ability to feel naturally energised and vibrant. Trust needs to be put back into the intelligence of our body to give us the power that we require without intervening.

The belief that can stop us from naturally relaxing to recharge can come from our family beliefs or work ethic, our community or industry beliefs, or our societal beliefs. A key indicator can be, as mentioned before, if you find you have to artificially gain energy or use something to relax, or if when you are relaxing you feel guilty and lazy. In no way am I saying that you should be lazy all the time, nor am I endorsing a sedentary lifestyle in general. The purpose, if your intention is to gain a natural high, is that you need to be able to relax in order to regain your momentum for the purposes of productivity, inspiration, creativity, extroversion and all the benefits of the natural high.

Of course, there can be circumstantial obstacles to having downtimes, such as children, a business, a career or other responsibilities that take a lot of attention and time. The great news is it's not always about longevity, but more so about the quality of the downtime. For example, you can spend a whole day 'relaxing' but your mind could be overly occupied, or you are constantly scrolling on your phone, so there is no actual mental downtime. Or, you could be mentally giving yourself downtime, but doing something physically strenuous the whole day and not get the recharge that you need.

We tend to spend so much time running around, getting through to-do lists in our heads, trying to suppress emotions in our relationships, overthinking, under-communicating - and the list goes on - that we actually think we are doing well because we are so busy (and tired), and we don't hesitate in telling people like it's a badge of honour. Should we feel proud that we are not able to relax and enjoy our lives? Does the person lying on the couch, not working but not financially stressed either, have a better internal life than the person who is overworked and stressed with no time for family?'

To really relax, you need to relax on all levels: mental, emotional, physical, and spiritual. This may look different on different days, weeks, or months - but a general combination will be optimal for restoration, and worthwhile time invested. Some ways in which you can do this, either in combination or together, are:

Spending time during the day to lie down, whether it be floating in a bath, lying on the grass or sand, or laying on a bed or couch Daydreaming by letting your mind wander and allowing your imagination to take over, without focusing on something outside in your physical reality

Meditation, either through sitting in a quiet place, mindfully breathing and allowing your thoughts to go past like clouds, or

sitting or lying down listening to guided meditations with specific focuses (there are thousands available for free online on YouTube or you can listen to ours on our app Heal)

Journalling through freestyle writing when feeling negative emotions can get your repetitive negative thoughts out of your head and onto paper for contemplation or emotional release (you'll get taken through this exercise in the last section of this book)

Extra sleep and power-napping, even a 5 to 15-minute nap during the day can help you to avoid unnecessary snacking or stimulants (which inevitably creates a crash later) and can allow you to feel refreshed for the rest of the day

Social relaxation, through actively listening and holding space for others. This takes the focus off you and onto others for an amount of time

Reading and researching, get you focused on learning and understanding rather than focusing on current stressors and problems.

These are just a few examples. Try a few different ones to experience the cause and effect of them. You will know what works best for you after you have tried them a few times and as you start to feel a surge of energy and motivation arise in you to do the things that you are inspired by, or to do tasks which are allowing you to work towards a goal - which you may not have had the energy to do so before.

If you feel you are procrastinating or sabotaging, then look at if you are actually inspired by your work and tasks, or what you are working towards. If you find that you are procrastinating on tasks that *need* to be done, like paying the bills, taking the bins out, and cleaning the sink (things that make it easier for your future self) then you can use a simple method that I have used over the years as follows:

Take two things that you need to do, but that you really don't want to do. Annoying tasks, like having to call the electricity company to amend a bill or some bookkeeping for your accountant. You know that not doing them will continue to stress you or weigh on your mind, always sitting on the back of your shoulders and draining energy away from your natural high, or inner peace.

So, right now, I want you to think of a few *undesirable tasks* that you know you need to do - but have been delaying. Think of the top two that need to be done.

Okay, now today (or tomorrow, but don't always make it tomorrow!) these are the only 2 things that you are allowed to do, aside from the basic needs of yourself and your family. No other tasks are more important. You are allowed to procrastinate, but only from task one to task two, or vice versa.

Try it and watch how quickly they get done!

16

The Future

> *Yesterday is gone. Tomorrow has not yet come.*
> *We have only today. Let us begin.*
> — Mother Theresa

So how do we move forward with all this? Now we are aware of what could be blocking us from peacefulness, and what we imagine people will think of us taking action at the moment, let's look at the future.

Our mind has an automatic habit of projecting scenarios into our future based on our past experiences. We can daydream and hope for better, but more often than not we just recreate our day-to-day through our usual patterns. Worry, fear, and anxiety are all just projecting the worst-case scenarios into our future. The reason we have physical symptoms from anxiety, for example, is because our body does not know whether we are imagining something in the future or recalling a memory - it thinks it's happening in the now and reacts accordingly. Our nervous system reacts like it's in danger. The more it is stressed and scared from past experiences, the more intense this will feel (from a scale of feeling a little nervous to possibly a panic attack).

So many people are on autopilot with this. Even I had been in the past. Not realise that I was just reacting to life, worried about what other people thought of me, which is really the root cause of anxiety and depression. Not feeling like we are enough for the world, not enough or perfect *just as we are*. But we *are* and we deserve to be free and peaceful - that is our true nature.

I would like to share a technique that will allow you to perhaps tap into this part of yourself. The part of you which is abundant in energy, love, and wisdom (without needed drugs or behaviours of course) - Our soul.

If you find it hard to memorise the following steps - you might have to have someone read this to you while your eyes are shut, or you can find a recording of this by searching 'The Awareness Technique The Centre for Healing' on YouTube *(make sure you subscribe too!)*:

Close your eyes.
Take a few deep breaths into your belly. Relax your shoulders, and unclench your jaw.
Now ask, in your mind...
"I wonder what my brain will think of next?"
Now breathe into that space

What happened to you, what did you experience?

The most common response I hear from people is 'nothing', but this is exactly the point of what I am trying to show you. Perhaps you experienced a slowing down, or gap in your thoughts? A moment in time where, just for a few seconds, there was no thought. Then I'd like to ask you: "So who is normally looking at, listening to or being aware of the thoughts?"

So often people make the mistake of thinking that they are their thoughts, or that their thoughts are completely real or true. Couple this with emotion and it easily turns into behaviour or action... perhaps regrettable ones sometimes.

Then the regrets, hurts and pain starts to accumulate... and you know the story.

Once we allow ourselves to step back and become a witness to our thoughts, we know they are just bubbling up from somewhere deeper in the mind, perhaps trying to protect us or blame others. The voice tells us to do the thing that we promised ourselves that we would stop doing, which keeps creating negativity in our lives. What if instead we could become curious, step back from our thoughts and find them interesting - wonder where they are coming from - rather than taking action on them? This is essentially what mindfulness is!

Thoughts are not instructions for us; we are not robots. Our thoughts are helpful if and when our mind is used as a tool.

Remember, you are an awareness, a witness. Sit with this for a moment and see if it resonates for you. Even the words in this book, it's just my experience and research from over the years, as if you are reading my thoughts. I really want you to practice discernment. Is it true for you - does it resonate? Does it challenge you to grow? Think critically. Don't be like those people that watch the news and negativity, take it on board and then create drama and negativity in their own lives. Why? Because we create our futures in our minds. We give our minds these subtle instructions by what we feed it, by our past experiences, and it goes about trying to help you fulfil those.

Picturing or predicting a worst-case scenario in the future? There will be an ongoing stream of worries, negative self-talk, thoughts, behaviours, and feelings - all in an effort to fulfil the negative.

Creating or deciding on having hope for a future that you choose? Then again, your mind will respond like a computer and set about making it a reality for you, making sure your filter of reality will highlight opportunities and things that support what you want.

Can you have a combination of both? For sure. We are complex beings.

Being aware of your future is the first step to ensuring you can start creating it. Noticing when negative thoughts arise, acknowledging them, reframing them if need be or seeking help if it's ongoing and affecting your ability to be present in the stream of consciousness (the gateway to the natural high).

I ONCE HAD A CLIENT WHO HAD BEEN SABOTAGING HIS RELATIONSHIP WITH

HIS WIFE AND HIS FAMILY. HE WAS CHEATING ON HER AND TAKING DRUGS - AND EASILY GETTING CAUGHT OUT, HENCE WHY HE ENDED UP AT OUR REHAB CENTRE. PART OF HIM SEEMED TO REALLY WANT TO STOP, BUT A STRONGER PART OF HIM WAS STILL DOING THESE ACTS THAT WERE LEADING THEM TO SEPARATION. AS EXPECTED, THE PEOPLE INVOLVED TAKE IT PERSONALLY AND THINK MAYBE THEY ARE NOT GOOD ENOUGH FOR THE PERSON TO COMMIT TO THEM AND STAY CLEAN, BUT IT IS NOT USUALLY ABOUT THAT AT ALL - WHICH

WE WENT ON TO DISCOVER. WE WENT THROUGH THE FUTURE HEALING PROTOCOL OF THE ROOT-CAUSE

THERAPY METHOD. IT TOOK US TO AN EVENT IN HIS FUTURE. HE HAD AN INTERNAL IMAGE OF LOOKING INSIDE HIS HOUSE, WITH HIS FAMILY HAPPY INSIDE. HE WAS OUTSIDE, JUST LOOKING IN AND FEELING SAD AND ALONE AND NOT FEELING PART OF THE FAMILY ANYMORE. IT IS AS IF HE HAD CREATED SUCH A STRONG NEGATIVE GOAL IN HIS MIND,

A DIRECTION THAT HIS MIND AND BODY HAVE BEEN GIVEN STRONG INSTRUCTIONS FOR, WHICH HE MUST TAKE ACTION ON TO ACHIEVE. THIS GOAL HE HAD EMBEDDED AND EXPECTED IN HIS FUTURE WAS THE CAUSE OF HIS REBELLIOUS AND SABOTAGING BEHAVIOUR IN THE RECENT PAST AND NOW. I ASSISTED HIM IN PROCESSING AND RELEASING THESE EMOTIONS TO LEARN AND GAIN CLARITY AND, POSITIVELY, THE FUTURE EVENT CHANGED TO HIS ACTUAL HEARTS DESIRE, WHICH WAS TO WALK IN AND JOIN THEM, AS THEY LOOKED UP AT HIM WITH LOVE AND WELCOMING ARMS.

The more we heal our layers, and conditioning, forgive the past and release the future to remember who we truly are, the greater access to this natural high and safety in the presence of now.

M.K HIEMANN

17

Relax

> *Tension is who you think you should be. Relaxation is who you are.* –Chinese Proverb

It may feel conflicting if now I mention to you that the whole point of the natural high or labelling these teachings to you anyway, is actually all about feeling safe to relax, about finding inner peace and being aligned with your purpose or contribution to the world.

I won't lie, finding this safety at the moment can be a journey that takes many years. Myself, I have been working on this for over half a decade now and can still find triggers, disturbances, and inner conflict - it's a relentless journey of finding and peeling back more layers. I catch myself when my mind wants to wander into the future or the past, and like a fishing rod reel, I need to catch myself and bring my awareness back into the present moment. If I find I have caught a snag, and no matter how many times I try and reel it in, it gets stuck, then I know I need to look into what is happening on a deeper level.

These deeper levels of the mind are calling to you through your thoughts and emotions, asking for integration and healing. Especially if your intention and goal are to find more inner peace.

So I ask you now, how safe do you feel relaxing into this very moment? To be completely present with your thoughts and how you are feeling? Are you able to

sit with uncomfortableness within your body, or is it too overwhelming and you find you automatically want to push it down and escape?

A relaxation technique is any method, process, procedure, or activity that helps a person to relax; attain a state of increased calmness; or otherwise reduce levels of pain, anxiety, stress, or anger.
- Wikipedia

If we are to understand the overall goal - feeling relaxed and satisfied within ourselves - we need to look at what the opposite is. Just like when we want to overcome something fully and learn, we need to experience it and grow through it.

Things to dive into to overcome, rather than to avoid (these are in my own words from my own experience with myself and assisting others only, and are not meant for diagnosis):

Frustration - When reality is different from what we desire. Ask yourself if you are being realistic about what you are wanting at that moment.

Stress - When you feel you cannot control a situation which causes you to feel worried about your needs being met or losing something.

Depression - Anger and shame turned towards the self, causing low energy and
sadness.

Physical Pain - Caused by a physical accident. If ongoing, a need for the emotional pain memory to be released.

Anger - A cover emotion or guard against fear or hurt.

Anxiety - Not feeling safe in the moment due to past trauma and projecting the unsafety into the future through the nervous system.

Or substances:

Alcohol - To seek safety and comfort from neglect and the anger/anxiety that it constantly creates.

Cigarettes - To push down guilt or grief, also to keep ourselves 'doing' as we've
been taught that it's lazy to relax.

Marijuana - To escape reality and our overthinking. Needing more nurturing. *Methamphetamine* - To push through when we feel like giving up. To forget the shame and to feel like we are achieving something.

Cocaine - To give us confidence, because if we lose face, we lose everything.

Heroin - because we have never felt or have forgotten what it is like to feel real love.

I ask you to take in the above, sit with it and see where some, or all, of these, are playing out in your life. Become aware and conscious about what is going on for you internally, no matter what is going on externally. Once you are *aware*, you can start to dive deeper into *why* and start to notice what you can and cannot change.

Can you change how you are looking at something? Can you take action to tick something off the list that has been in the back of your mind for a long time? Can you start to forgive yourself and others and let go of those flashbacks that drop in and disturb your peace?

I will leave you with one last analogy, a framework for ensuring the goal is clear and that you have a frame of reference to aim towards in this life journey.

Imagine your mind is like a battery. It only has so much charge. When a device is complex and is doing a lot of functions at once, the battery loses power quickly because it spreads and distributes its energy so far. Now imagine your mind and body as this device. The more internal conflicts we have, the more we're holding onto, trying to remember, keep alive, and the pains we haven't forgiven and cannot let go of, and the more our energy is spread out and not focused and strong.

Now think of the same battery, focusing its energy on one task at a time, methodically. All of a sudden there is so much more charge available and the tasks at hand get done completely, powerfully and almost in a joy-like state.

How can you organise and create your life so you can focus on one thing at a time? Being completely present with what you are doing - your work, your children and your loved ones.

Lastly, it has been my absolute honour that you have taken this journey and precious time in your life to read this book.

Please, if you found value in this, share and recommend it to those you love. Let's heal the world together, one person at a time.

I welcome you to contact one of our qualified practitioners or if you are interested in becoming a healer in the methodology that we use and love, please visit www.thecentreforhealing.com to find out more.

M.K HIEMANN

JOURNAL EXERCISE

As a last note,
I invite you to try the following as a self-healing tool:

Please feel free to use the last pages of this book as your own journal for the purposes of this exercise. The way that I teach journalling isn't likely the same as what you may have been taught previously - or you may have never tried and thoughts of 'dear diary' come to mind.

This is the method of journalling that we often teach our clients. It's a way to start processing and releasing low vibrational emotions and energy and gain wisdom from your intuition, returning to a sense of feeling balanced on the other side.

FOR EXAMPLE. ONE DAY I WOKE UP FEELING SO PHYSICALLY AND EMOTIONALLY HEAVY AND TIRED. I COULD NOT WORK OUT WHY I WAS FEELING THAT WAY AND I HAD A LOT THAT I WANTED TO DO THAT DAY. SO, I GRABBED MY NOTEBOOK AND STARTED WRITING ALL OF THE NEGATIVE THOUGHTS THAT WERE COMING TO MIND,

JOURNAL EXERCISE

ALL OF THE FEELINGS AND FRUSTRATION. UPON WRITING MY DARKEST AND DEEPEST, MOST UGLY THOUGHTS, IN VERY RECKLESS MESSY HANDWRITING... IT TURNED UP THE NEGATIVE EMOTION. I WAS NO LONGER RESISTING IT BUT LETTING IT TAKE OVER, FULLY FACING IT. AS I TURNED UP THE EMOTION AND AS IT STARTED TO SUBSIDE (AS THAT IS WHAT EMOTIONS ARE MEANT TO DO - MOVE THROUGH US LIKE A WAVE FOR FEEDBACK, TO TELL US WHETHER WE ARE ON OR OFF PATH - BUT SO OFTEN THEY HAVE BEEN STUCK BECAUSE WE HAVEN'T FELT SAFE TO EXPRESS IN THE MOMENT, OR HAVE MADE AN ASSUMPTION OR STORY ABOUT WHAT WAS HAPPENING AND FELT RESISTANT TO IT - YES MANY REASONS!)... I THEN GOT A GLIMPSE OF THE REASON WHY.

THE FEEDBACK THAT IT WAS TRYING TO SHOW ME. A CLEARER PERCEPTION.

AS THE EMOTION WENT DOWN, THE WORDS AUTOMATICALLY CAME OUT ONTO THE NOTEBOOK: "I FEEL ASHAMED ABOUT MY MONEY SITUATION". AS I CONTINUED TO WRITE MY FRUSTRATIONS, THEY CONTINUED TO GO DOWN UNTIL THE FEELING COMPLETELY SUBSIDED. THEN THE WISDOM DROPPED IN. I WAS CREATING UNREALISTIC EXPECTATIONS OF MYSELF, AND NOT TRUSTING.

JOURNAL EXERCISE

MY ENERGY COMPLETELY CAME BACK, I WENT BACK TO FEELING DRIVEN AND PEACEFUL AND WENT ON WITH MY DAY AS USUAL. IT COMPLETELY SHIFTED AND I WAS OUT OF THE FUNK. SO, WHETHER YOU GET THE UNDERSTANDING RIGHT AWAY, OR LATER IN
THE DAY, IT'S A TRULY LIBERATING EXPERIENCE.

Feel free to use the following pages, go ahead and give it a try!

JOURNAL

JOURNAL

JOURNAL

JOURNAL

NOTES

Melissa Hiemann NLPP. CH.t TLTP RC.t ADV.DIP INTBUS is the Director of The Centre for Healing, which she Co-founded with her now partner Ryan Hassan in 2016.

After spending most of her young adult life battling undiagnosed anxiety from trauma through self-medicating and partying, she finally sought help from an alternative therapist. Having experienced the life-changing benefits - she felt deeply that she had found her purpose and way to help others and proceeded to study and then open her own practice in 2014.

She has since made it her life's work, around raising her son and travelling the world with her partner Ryan Hassan, both personally and professionally to assist people to understand and be set free from their negative emotions and any self-imposed limitations that are holding them back from feeling peaceful and living a full life on purpose.

She is the creator and registered trainer of Root-cause Therapy and Trauma-Informed Manifestation Coaching, which she teaches to students all around the world through the online healing centre. This therapy has been an accumulation of many other modalities that she has tested and experienced, along with daily research and meditation for over half a decade in an effort to bring the most innovative ways to society to heal trauma in a complete and safe manner.

She, along with her life partner Ryan has a goal to change the way that practitioners treat mental health and addictions, and are advocates and change-makers in healing the root-cause, rather than just treating the symptoms through sharing their methods with the aim to *heal the world, one person at a time.*

www.ingramcontent.com/pod-product-compliance
Lightning Source LLC
Chambersburg PA
CBHW070308010526
44107CB00056B/2523